The Colouring Book of EDINBURGH

by
Eilidh Muldoon

BIRLINN

Edinburgh Castle

Grassmarket

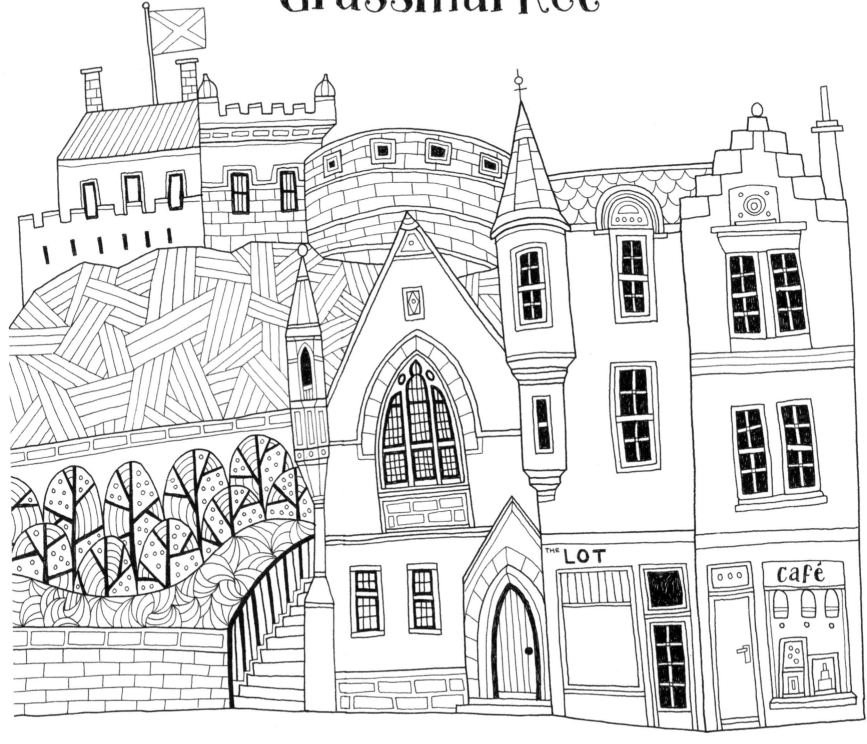

National Museum of Scotland

Greyfriars

The Meadows

Dynamic Earth

Scottish Parliament

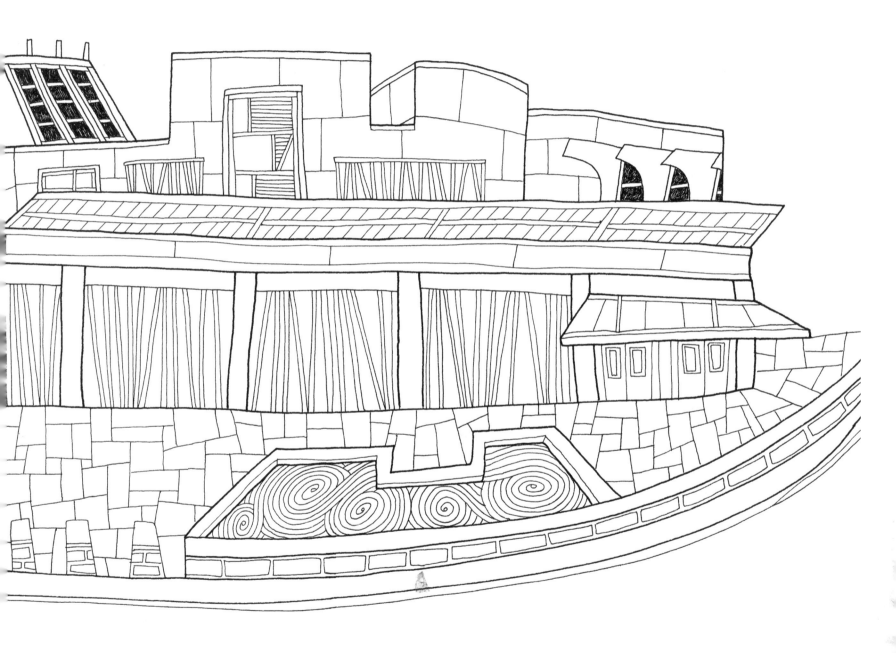

The Royal Mile

Tron Kirk

ST GILES CATHEDRAL

St Giles Cathedral

Ramsay Garden

The Usher Hall

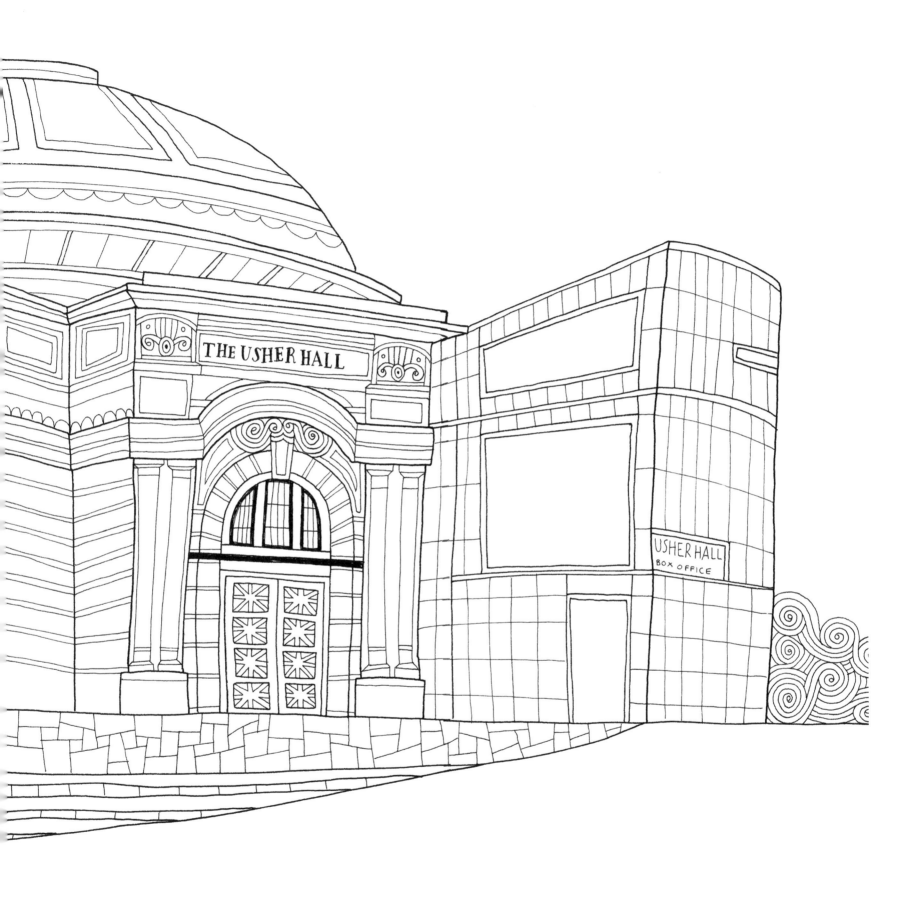

Edinburgh Zoo

Dean Village

Charlotte Square

Royal Botanic Garden

The Shore, Leith

Princes Street

Balmoral Hotel

Calton Hill

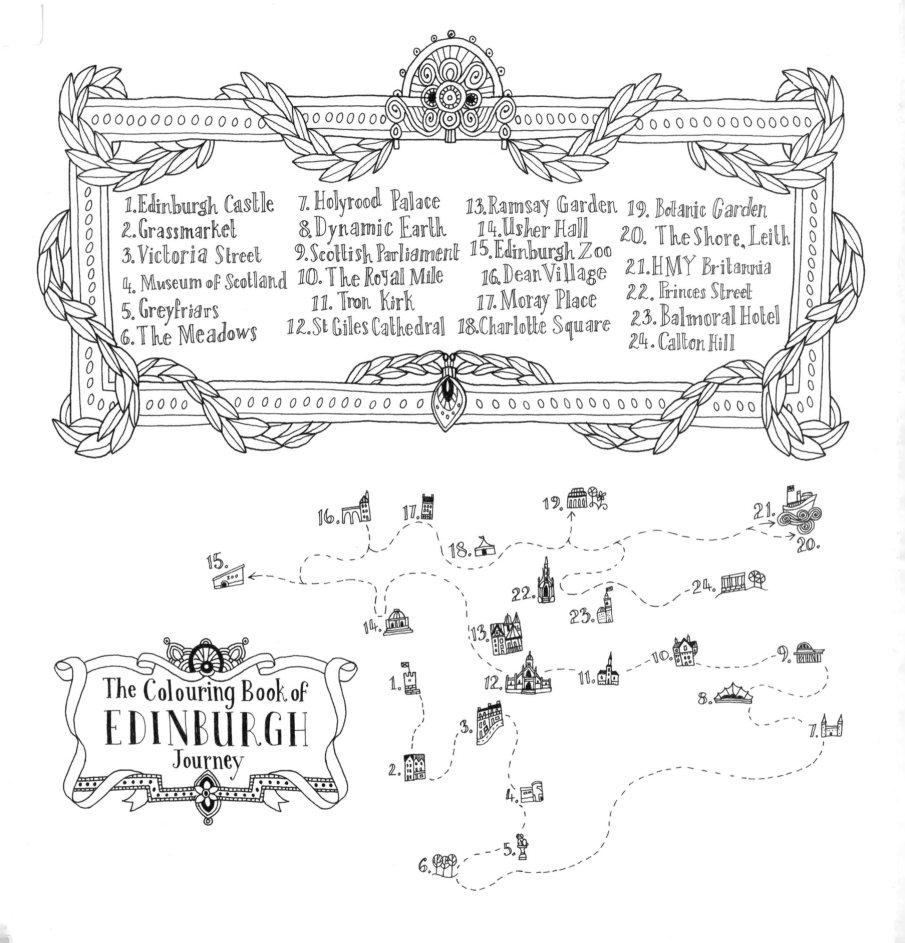

1. Edinburgh Castle
2. Grassmarket
3. Victoria Street
4. Museum of Scotland
5. Greyfriars
6. The Meadows
7. Holyrood Palace
8. Dynamic Earth
9. Scottish Parliament
10. The Royal Mile
11. Tron Kirk
12. St Giles Cathedral
13. Ramsay Garden
14. Usher Hall
15. Edinburgh Zoo
16. Dean Village
17. Moray Place
18. Charlotte Square
19. Botanic Garden
20. The Shore, Leith
21. HMY Britannia
22. Princes Street
23. Balmoral Hotel
24. Calton Hill

The Colouring Book of
EDINBURGH
Journey